Knit an
Enchanted Castle

CW00919908

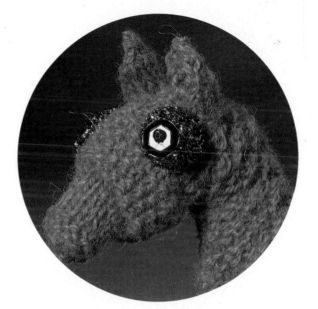

Knit an
Enchanted Castle

Jan Messent

SEARCH PRESS

Introduction

Enter the world of enchantment, the world of witches and wizards, dragons and unicorns, bold knights on horseback and talking trees. Inside the huge stone castle lives the handsome prince who will one day find his beautiful princess and take her to live there in safety. Well, that's the beginning of the story. What happens along the way can be created with the help of an active imagination, some knitting needles, yarn, these patterns and a little time and patience. These little figures are made to a scale of about 5 in (14 cm) tall, and while we think that many people, both young and old, will enjoy having them in their possession, the wire frames make them unsuitable as toys for very young children. Their real function is to bring back the world of make-believe in a truly three-dimensional way and to delight anyone with a sense of fantasy and appreciation of fairy-tales. Judging by the popularity of Tolkein's books, plenty of people come under that heading.

The clothes *can* be made removeable, though in the patterns they fit tightly without fastenings. However, the instructions are not complex as most pieces are rectangular or triangular shapes; even the castle is made from straight pieces of knitting and would be an excellent piece for a group of people to make together.

Materials

Needles: exact requirements are given in the instructions for each character, but generally, very fine needles are used throughout. These are sometimes easier to find in sets of four double-pointed ones, rather than in pairs. These are perfectly adequate as only a few stitches are used on most projects. Other requirements are stitch-holders and row-counters, and blunt-ended needles for sewing with wool (tapestry needles). You may also need a fine crochet hook.

Yarns: very small amounts of two-ply baby yarns, three-ply, four-ply and some double-knitting (D.K.) for the castle and trees. See the individual patterns for exact requirements. The colours are your personal choice. You will need a thick yarn for wrapping round the frames of figures, and oddments of other colours too, for embroidering features and other details. Glittering metallic yarns are especially useful.

Wire: pipe-cleaners are used as the framework for the characters, but for the trees, a stronger, bendable wire will be needed. You may also need wire cutters and a small pair of pliers.

Padding and card: padding is needed for the animals and talking trees, also cardboard tubes (insides of toilet rolls), others about 9–10 in (23 cm) long and small pieces of thick card for stands. Other requirements for the castle are given under that heading.

Extras: all kinds of extras may be added as the fancy takes you; the knight, for instance, carries a shield made of card but could also have a sword as well as a lance. Beads, buckles, sequins and gold cords all add a touch of sparkle and magic, so look into your bit-box. Whatever is small enough will probably have a use. You may also need small amounts of glue and sticky tape.

Sizes and tensions

Please note that all instructions are *general indications* and will almost certainly have to be altered here and there to fit figures of all shapes and sizes, as no two people ever produce exactly the same shape. You may have to add or subtract a few stitches and/or a few rows, and if a different yarn is used from the one recommended, then a bit of juggling is inevitable! *Do* measure your knitted pieces against the figure you have made to make sure that each bit fits before you sew it up.

Stitches and abbreviations

Most of the items are knitted in stocking stitch (abbreviated to s.s.) made by knitting and purling alternate rows. The other side of this is known as reverse stocking stitch (rev.s.s.) Garter stitch is made by knitting every row. Other abbreviations are as follows:

alt.	alternate
beg.	beginning
cm	centimetre
ch	crochet chain
dec.	decrease
d.c.	double crochet (American equivalent, single crochet)
foll.	following
gm.	gramme
in	inch
inc.	increase
k.	knit
k2tog.	knit 2 sts together to decrease
L.H.	left hand
L.S.	left side
M1	make one st. by picking up the strand between 2 needles and knitting into it
mm.	millimetre
p2tog.	purl 2 sts together to decrease
patt.	pattern
p.c.	pipe cleaner
psso	pass the slipped stitch over
p.	purl
p.wise	purlwise
rem.	remaining
R.H.	right hand
R.S.	right side
sl.	slip
sl.st.	slip stitch
st.	stitch
t.b.l.	through back of loop
W.S.	wrong side
y.fwd.	yarn forward
y.o.n.	yarn on needle
y.r.n.	yarn round needle

THE STITCHES USED

Stocking stitch
Garter stitch
Single rib
Moss stitch
Double moss stitch
Others of own choice for the castle walls

Making a wire frame body

The basic framework for most of the characters featured in this book is simple to make, (see Fig 1).

(1) Two pipe-cleaners are laid together and twisted as shown to make the head and arms.

(2) Loop another p.c., slip it over the head and twist it to make the top of the legs and body.

(3) Loop another p.c. in half and slip it over the head on the other side so that one loop lies to the front and the other to the back. Twist these and also the tops of the legs. Do a bit of pulling and tugging at this stage to ensure that the arms do not get pushed too far down the frame and look as if they come from the middle of the body.

(4) Make two legs as follows: one p.c. bent double, bend up about ½ in (1 cm) at the folded end to form the foot. Lay this leg-section alongside the leg which is attached to the body, so that the overall height measures no more than 4½ in (11 cm). Bind the 2 leg-pieces together with sticky tape. Turn up the arms to make them equal length.

(5) Bind the head, body and arms with thick pink yarn, sewing the ends into the body and wrapping around the neck tightly as shown.

fig 1

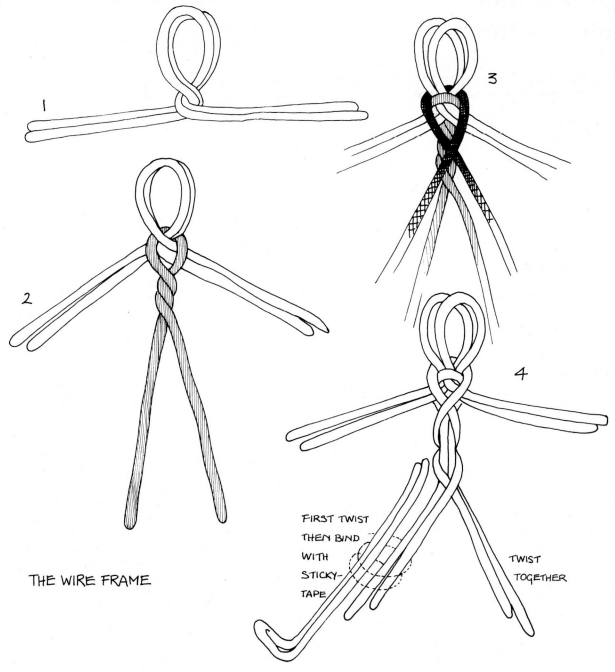

1

2

3

4

THE WIRE FRAME

FIRST TWIST
THEN BIND
WITH
STICKY-
TAPE

TWIST
TOGETHER

6

Knitted body covering

(6) Begin with the head and knit in s.s. throughout. Use 2 ply baby-yarn and size 1½ mm. needles, or finer. You will need about 20 sts. for the head covering, and about 18 rows to make a piece which continues down past the neck and well on to the shoulders. Gather the last sts. on to a thread and draw these up to form the top of the head as shown. Sew the seam up the back and run a tight gathering thread around the neck. Sew the cast-on edge to the shoulder area.

Make legs on about 10 sts. as long as necessary for each figure to the top of the leg. Draw the last sts. up on to a length of yarn and gather. Sew up the seam, and sew on to the complete leg.

For the arms, you will need about 10 sts. As with the legs, the pieces are not cast off but gathered on to the ends of the limbs. Attach the arm-pieces well up on to the shoulder covering.

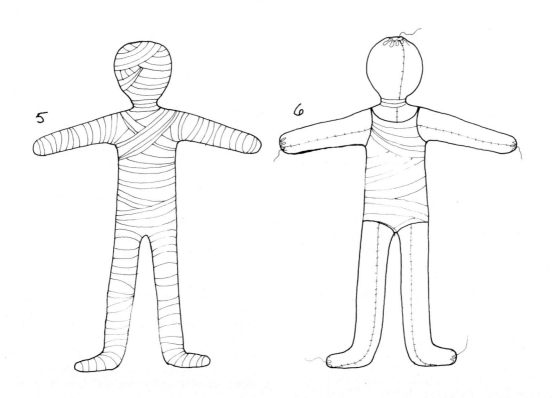

The prince

The handsome and charming prince of all the best stories wears eighteenth-century style dress, tight breeches tucked into tall riding boots, a fitted jacket edged with gold, the lace cuffs and cravat show at wrists and neck, and on his natural brown curls, (tied back with a ribbon), he wears a three-cornered hat from which hangs a plume of feathers. The shirt, to make less bulk under the jacket, takes the form of a vest-front, so the lace cuffs are added to the sleeves of his jacket, see photo on page 9.

MATERIALS

Needles: 2 mm. for all pieces. You may also find a 2.50 mm. crochet hook useful.
Yarn: small amounts of 3 ply in deep yellow, white, gold metallic, brown for boots, hair and eyes, a short length of fluffy yarn for feathers, and smooth pink for the mouth.
Extras: beads for buttons, and sequins for extra sparkle if required.

BREECHES AND BOOTS (all in one piece)

Beginning at the waist and using deep yellow yarn, cast on 10 sts. and work in s.s. for 25 rows. On the next row, dec. 1 st. at each end to make 8 sts. Change to brown for boots, and continue in s.s. for 18 rows, or until long enough to reach the end of the foot. Draw the sts. up on to a threaded needle and sew up as far as the top of the boot. Make another piece the same. Sew centre back and centre front seams, slip on to the body, putting the feet into the boots, and sew down the legs. The boots may have a gold band embroidered round the tops. Darn all ends in.

SHIRT FRONT AND CRAVAT

This is simply an oblong of s.s. (10 sts., 13 rows), in fine white 3 ply. On the 14th row: knit. 15th row: purl. 16th row: knit, then cast off p.wise. These last rows form the neck edge. Sew this piece to the front of the body to slightly overlap the top of the breeches.

For the cravat, make 2 separate pieces and sew the narrow edges to the neck band of the shirt. Cast on 8 sts. and work in single rib for 5 rows.
Next row: (k2tog.) 4 times.
Next row: k.
Next row: p., then cast off k.wise.

The second piece is the same except that the last 2 rows are omitted. This piece is sewn on top of the other.

COAT

Begin at the lower edge, and with deep yellow yarn, cast on 22 sts. and work in single rib for 10 rows.
Next row: (k2tog. k.8) twice, k2tog.
Next row: p.
Next row: k2tog., k.6, k2tog., k.7, k2tog., (16 sts.).
Next row: p.

Continue in s.s. until the under-arm division for the sleeves, (i.e. about 4 more rows)
Next row: work on the first 4 sts. for 7 rows.

Break off yarn and rejoin it to the centre 8 sts. Work 7 rows. Break yarn and rejoin to the last 4 sts. and work 7 rows, then p. across all 16 sts. P. one more row, k. the next and cast off p.wise.

With gold metallic yarn, work an edge of crochet all the way round the coat beginning at the centre of the back edge.

SLEEVES (make 2)

Cast on 10 sts. and work 8 rows in s.s.
9th row: p., then break off yarn and change to white (as for shirt).
10th row: p., and cast off p.wise.

This makes a tiny white cuff on to which the lace ruffle is crocheted, so do not break the yarn, but using a 2.50mm. hook, crochet a frill along this edge as follows:
Next row: *3 ch., 1 dc. into next ch.sp. * to end.
You may knit this frill if you prefer.

Darn in unwanted ends at this stage and sew the lace cuff with rem. white yarn. Sew up the rest of the sleeve and slide it on to the arm, placing the seam at

OPPOSITE
The handsome prince carries the princess away on his white horse and they live happily ever after.

the back. With metallic yarn, embroider a whip stitch over the p. row along the cuff edge. Sew the sleeve to the coat armhole.

HAIR AND FACE

Using mottled brown yarn, cast on 14 sts. and work in g.st. for 10 rows. Over the next 4 rows, k2tog. at each end to make 6 sts., (i.e. on alt. rows).

Work in single rib for 8 rows on these 6 sts., then cast off in rib. Gather the cast-on edge with a running st. and sew up to form the crown of the head. Embroider the face, and then sew the hair on to the head. Make a ribbon of crochet chain and tie this round the bunch of hair at the nape of the neck.

THREE-CORNERED HAT

For the crown of the hat, cast on 14 sts. and work 4 rows in s.s. Gather the last row and sew up the seam.

For the brim, cast on 16 sts. and work 2 rows in s.s. then * k.1, inc in next st., repeat from * to the end of the row, (24 sts.).
Next row: p.
Next row: * k.1, inc. in next st., repeat from * to the end of the row, (36 sts.).
Next row: p.
Last row: k., then cast off p.wise and sew up the 2 short edges.

Sew the cast-on edge of the brim to the cast-on edge of the crown, then fold up the brim to make 3 points at equal distances. Sew to the crown in the centre of each side (do not sew right along to the point, but run the needle through the crown to the centre of each side) with a few firm sts. Sew the hat to the head with one point at the front. The feathers are made from a crochet chain about 4 in (10 cm) long sewn into a bunch . Fluffy yarn is best for this.

The princess

The princess can be made to match your own individual ideas of what an enchanting princess should look like, colour of hair, clothes, and so on. This one wears a circlet of (crochet chain) glittery yarn over her auburn shoulder-length hair, a deep blue embroidered gown (actually the pattern is knitted in) over an underskirt of white lace. If this appears to be too "holey" you may have to make another white layer beneath that, as I have done. This is simply an oblong gathered at the waist. The frilly white collar and sleeve ruffles, and the sparkling slippers complete the outfit, see photo on page 9.

MATERIALS

Needles: 2¼ mm. and a 2.50 mm. crochet hook.
Yarns: 3 ply blue and white, a glittery yarn for the circlet, and a blue metallic yarn for the skirt pattern, and slippers. Brown (auburn) yarn for hair and oddments for features.

WHITE UNDERSKIRT AND VEST

The vest is a tiny oblong of rev. s.s., (8 sts., 5 rows), sewn across the front of the body.

For the underskirt, cast on 50 sts. and work about 30 rows altogether, but to obtain the lacy effect, make half of this amount in picot st. or any other simple lacy st.

(Picot st is made on 2 rows: * k2tog., y.fwd. repeat from * to end of row, then p. the next row. This makes a row of holes.)

The next-to-the-last row of the skirt should be decreased as follows: k2tog. all across the row to make 25 sts., then p. the last row and cast off. Join the 2 side edges, gather the top, fit on to the waist, and sew in place.

BLUE DIVIDED OVERSKIRT

Cast on 70 sts. in blue yarn (A) and use metallic blue yarn as the secondary colour (B). [Note: for a simpler version, use plain s.s.]
Rows 1 & 2: use colour B and k.2 rows.
Row 3: A, (k.4, s1.2) to the last 4 sts., k.4
Row 4: A, (p.4, sl.2 p.wise) to the last 4 sts., p.4.
Rows 5 & 6: as rows 3 & 4.
Rows 7 & 8: B, k. all sts.
Row 9: A, k.1, (sl.2, k.4) to last 3 sts., sl.2, k.1.
Row 10: A, p.1, (sl.2 p.wise, p.4) to last 3 sts., sl.2, p.1.
Rows 11 & 12: as rows 9 & 10.

Repeat these 12 rows once more, then rows 1 & 2 again. Work 2 rows in A (s.s.).

Continue working in s.s. and dec. on the k. rows as follows:

Next row: (k.5, k2tog.) 10 times.

Next and alt. rows: p.

Next row: (k2tog., k.4) 10 times, (50 sts.).

Continue in s.s. on these sts. until the waistline is reached, then k2tog. all along the row (25 sts.), then p. one row. Cast off. Press the bottom edge *very gently* under a damp cloth to prevent it rolling up.

BODICE

Begin at the lower back (see Fig 2), cast on 9 sts. and work in s.s. for 8 rows.

9th row: k.2, cast off 5, k.2

Work on the 2 sets of 2 sts. for 3 rows, then inc. 1 st. on the inside edge (i.e. the neck edge) on *alternate* rows until there are 5 sts. on each side. P. one more row and cast off.

MAKING UP

Gather the skirt waistband to fit the figure closely,

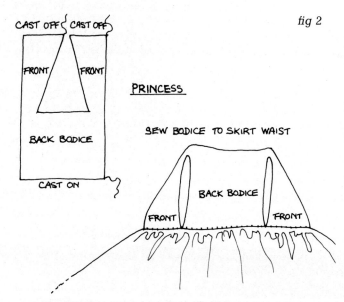

fig 2

PRINCESS

SEW BODICE TO SKIRT WAIST

SLIP THE BODICE AND SKIRT ON TO THE FIGURE AND STITCH THE TWO FRONT EDGES ONTO THE WHITE VEST.

leaving a gap of about ¼ in (6 mm) at the front. Do not sew on to the figure at this stage. Now follow the instructions on the diagram.

SLEEVES (make 2)

With blue yarn, cast on 20 sts. and work in s.s. for 4 rows.

5th row: k2tog. across all sts. to make 10 sts.

6th row: p.

Change to blue metallic yarn, k. one row and cast off k. wise.

Sew up the side seam and gather the top edge to fit the armhole. Sew this in place on to the bodice, pushing the sleeve edge up on to the "elbow". Now make a lace cuff as follows: with the fine white yarn, cast on 24 sts. and k. 2 rows, then k2tog. across all sts. to make 12. Cast off.

Gather the cast off edge, sew up the side edges, and then stitch the lace cuff to the sleeve edge.

LACE COLLAR

With the same yarn as the cuffs, cast on 40 sts. and k. 2 rows. Picot st. for 2 rows.

Next row: p2tog. across all sts. to make 20 sts. and cast off k.wise.

Sew cast-off edge to dress, (see Fig 2).

SHOES

Use blue metallic yarn, cast on 8 sts. and work in s.s. until long enough to slip over the foot (about 10 rows). Sew up the heel and gather the last row on to a thread and draw up over the toe. Sew this on to the foot.

HAIR AND FACE

Using brown (auburn) yarn for hair, cast on 16 sts. and work 4 rows in g.st.

5th row: p.

6th row: (k2tog., k.5) twice, k2tog., (13 sts.).

Work the next 13 rows in s.s. then gather all sts. tog. on a thread and draw up. Stitch this part to the top of the head, sew down the edges to the face and along the nape of the neck above the g.st. edge.

Embroider the face.

The tiara, or circlet, is a crochet chain of glittery yarn made into a cirle and stitched to the hair.

The knight

As the entire body is encased in shining armour, only the face requires a pink cover with embroidered eyes. For this, use a fine 2 ply dark flesh-coloured yarn on size 2 mm. needles, and work on 22 sts. for 14 rows. Gather the last sts. for the top of the head. The colour used on the cloak, shield and plume should all be the same, and if he rides on horseback, the trappings and harness should also be the same. The suit of armour is made from two main pieces; the helmet and tunic all-in-one, and the trousers and feet together. Any metallic colour will look good, gold, silver or bluish-silver. The helmet has another piece added on top of the 'hood' to give height, and this has a band of gold thread worked in. Measurements should be checked at all stages as yarns differ, see photo on page 12.

MATERIALS

Needles: 2 mm., 1½ mm.
Yarns: metallic yarn, small amounts of contrasting coloured 3 ply for cloak, plume, and eyes.
Extras: a small piece of thick card and one paper-stud for the shield. For the banner you will need a small lollipop stick and gold paper.

THE TROUSERS

These begin at the toe end. With metallic yarn and size 2 mm. needles, cast on 10 sts. and work in s.s. for 24 rows, then inc. 1 st. at each end of next row (12 sts.). Work 25 more rows and cast off. Make another piece the same.

Sew these 2 pieces together from the top as far as the top of the legs, slip this part on to the body and pin at the waist. Gather the 2 cast-on edges at the feet, and sew up the leg seams (with the legs inside). Stitch the waist edge to the body.

THE TUNIC AND UNDER-HELMET

These begin at the lower edge of the front. Use the same yarn and needles, and * cast on 14 sts. and work 2 rows in s.s. Work 2 rows of gold thread, then change back to silver for 2 rows. Dec. 1 st. at each end of the next row * and work 21 more rows, without shaping. 12 sts.

For the face-opening, k.3, cast off 6, k.3.

Work on the first set of 3 sts. for 7 rows in s.s., break the yarn and connect to the other 3 sts. and work 6 rows on these.

Next row: turn, cast on 5 sts., k. across the other 3 sts., (11 sts.).

P. across the complete row, working into the back of the 9th st. Work 2 more rows, gather sts. on to a thread and draw up.

For the back, work as for the front from * to *, then work 36 more rows, without shaping. Gather sts. on to a thread and draw up. Sew these 2 pieces tog. from the lower edges, leaving a space for the arms. Slip this on to the body, sew the shoulders and round the neck and on up to the under-helmet. Sew the face-opening round the face.

SLEEVE AND HAND (all in one)

Cast on 20 sts. and work 22 rows in s.s.

Do not cast off, gather the sts. on to a thread and fit this part on to the hands. Stitch up the sleeve seam and attach the tops to the armhole of the tunic. Make another in the same way.

THE HELMET

The extra helmet fits over the top of the other and pulls well down over the forehead. Cast on 22 sts. and work in g.st for 7 rows, the 3rd and 4th of these being in gold thread.
8th row: p.

Gather all sts. on to a thread and sew up the sides.

The plume is a thick, short tassel in the colours chosen for the other accessories. Sew it firmly to the top of the helmet and use a dab of glue of hold it in place at the back.

THE CLOAK

Gold 3 ply yarn was used for this but any other yarn will do as long as the measurements are checked

OPPOSITE
The brave silver knight and his horse are ready for battle.

against the figure. Using 1½ mm. needles, cast on 12 sts. and work 20 rows in s.s. At this point, introduce bands of colour (6 rows were used on the model) and on the last of these rows, 3 extra sts. were made, one at each end and one in the centre. (15 sts.). Work 4 more rows and cast off. Sew the top edge round the knight's neck.

THE SHIELD

This is a tiny shaped piece of gold card on to which has been glued a crochet circle of gold yarn. It is fastened to the knight's left arm with a paper stud which passes through the centre of the circle and curves round on to the arm behind, (see Fig 3 for actual size).

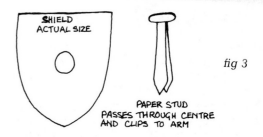

THE BANNER

Paint the lollipop stick silver. Cut a length of gold paper, fold and glue wrong sides together around the top of the pole, then cut out the banner shape.

The wizard

True to tradition, the wizard must *look* magical, and so he wears a long gown of bright colours and a tall pointed cap, though magicians do vary and you may have other ideas. His skin shows only on face and hands, as his legs and feet are covered in brown. The overgown takes the form of a long waistcoat, as the sleeves of this outer-garment and those of the under-gown are knitted in one piece. The overgown is split up the sides as far as the armholes, see photo on page 15.

MATERIALS

Needles: 2 mm. and 2¼ mm.
Yarns: small amounts of 3 ply turquoise for the undergown, and 3 ply random-dyed yarn for the overgown. If you cannot obtain this, try using a plain 3 ply together with a fine glittery yarn, but check the measurements as you go along. Red 3 ply was used for the hat (a very small amount), brown 3 ply for the legs and feet, metallic yarn for the buckle, white 2 ply for the hair and beard, and oddments for the features. 3 ply white yarn with a glitter thread running through it was used for the staff.

Extras: a large pretty sequin, or bead, for the jewel in the hat. You may like him to wear a heavy chain and jewel around his neck, or dress him in black and cover him in sparkling sequins. You will also need some glue.

OVERGOWN

Use 2¼ mm. needles and random-dyed yarn; begin at the back and cast on 18 sts. Work 32 rows in s.s., then cast off 3 sts. at beg. of next 2 rows. Dec. 1 st. at each end of foll 2 k. rows, (8 sts.). Work 5 more rows and leave these 8 sts. on a pin.

For the left front, cast on 9 sts. and work in s.s. for 32 rows but k. the last 2 sts. of every row. Cast off 3 sts. at beg of 33rd row. Dec. 1 st. at beg of next 2 k. rows. Work 6 more rows then leave these 4 sts. on a pin.

OPPOSITE
The wizard rests under the shade of the blossom tree.

For the right front, use the same instructions as for the left front *except* that the first 2 sts. of every row should be knitted. Reverse the armhole shaping. Place all three pieces back on to the needle (in the right order, armhole to armhole) and k. across all sts. (in g.st) for 4 rows, dec. at both ends of the last row, then cast off.

SLEEVES (make 2)

Darn all ends in, then with R.S. facing and random-yarn, pick up 22 sts. around the armhole and work 4 rows in s.s. and 2 rows in rev.s.s. Change to the same colour yarn as the undergown and p2tog. all along the row, (11 sts.). Work in s.s. to the wrist, about 3 rows, then cast off.

Darn ends in and press gently, sew up the lower sleeve edge and then the overgown sleeves, leaving about 2 in (5 cm) open up the sides of the gown.

UNDERGOWN

Cast on 16 sts. and work 24 rows in s.s. You may wish to insert a few rows of moss st here and there to add to the texture.

On the 25th row, k2tog. at both ends, and repeat this on the 27th, 29th and 31st row, (8 sts.).
P. alternate rows.

Continue in s.s. until the head is reached (about 10–12 rows) and cast off.

Make another piece in the same way. Press and sew up the side seams from the hem to ¾ in (2 cm) from the top. Slip the undergown on to the figure and sew up the shoulders. Now fit the overgown on top of this and decorate with a large buckle as folls: use gold metallic yarn and cast on 10 sts. Knit 3 rows in g.st. and cast off, then gather one long edge into a circle. Glue this in place.

BEARD

In the white yarn, and size 2 mm. needles, cast on 5 sts. and work in single rib for 6 rows. Inc. 1 st. at each end of the next 4 rows, (13 sts.).

Work 2 more rows in rib, then cast off in rib. Sew this round the lower face from ear to ear.

HAIR AND FACE

Cast on 20 sts. and work in single rib for 8 rows. Cast off in rib and sew one long edge around the head, leaving a bald patch on top. Embroider a pink nose, 2 blue eyes and thick white eyebrows.

HAT

Use 2¼ mm. needles and cast on 28 sts. Work 4 rows in s.s.
5th row: (k2tog., k.5) 4 times.
6th and alt rows: p.
7th row: (k2tog., k.4) 4 times.
9th row: (k2tog., k.3) 4 times.
11th row: (k2tog., k.2) 4 times.
13th row: (k2tog., k.1) 4 times, 8 sts.

Work 5 more rows in s.s. then (k.2 tog.) 4 times. Draw the last sts. on to a thread and sew up. Allow the brim to curl upwards at the front, and sew on to the head with a firm back st.

STAFF

1 p.c., doubled over at either end, will make the staff. Wrap tightly with the glittery yarn and sew it on to the wizard's hand.

The witch and her cat

Traditionally, witches appear in black and sombre colours, but our version is more colourful and wears a very dark purple over-dress which has lighter cuffs and border, and under this she wears a multi-coloured skirt over dark leg-coverings. Make her leg-coverings first, at the same time as her face and hand-covers. Then embroider her face (not too pretty) and knit her grey hair, as this helps to give her a certain character before you make her clothes. Keep her wrapped up warm while you're doing this, as witches get cross easily! See photo on page 18.

MATERIALS

Needles: 2 mm. and 2¼ mm.
Yarns: small amounts of dark purple 3 ply (or dark grey) for the over-dress and random-dyed yarn for the underskirt. Also small amounts of mid-purple and dark yarn for the dress and legs. Grey 3 ply for the hair and black for the hat. Oddments of yarns for the features.

The cat is made in rev. s.s. in dark charcoal, 3 ply, and a tiny amount of green will be needed for the eyes and white for the whiskers.
Extras: for the broomstick you will need oddments of brown yarn and thin wire.

HAIR AND HAT (all in one piece)

Begin with the hair; using grey yarn and 2¼ mm. needles, cast on 22 sts. and work in single rib for 12 rows.
Row 13: k2tog. all along the row, (11 sts.).
Row 14: change to black yarn and p.one row.

Continue in s.s. as follows for the top of the hat: work 6 rows straight, then (k2tog., k.1) to last 2 sts., k2tog. Work 3 rows straight, then (k2tog.) 3 times to last st., k.1. P. one row, then (k2tog.) twice. Cast off.

Sew up the black point, leaving the grey hair open to frame the face. Now make the brim as follows: with black yarn, cast on 30 sts. and k.3 rows.
Next row: (k.1, k2tog.) 10 times, then k. one more row.
Next row: (k2tog., k.3) 4 times. Cast off loosely.

Sew up the 2 short sides to form a circle. Stitch the hair on to the witch's head, pulling it well down, then slip the brim over and sew, making sure that no grey hair shows on top.

UNDERSKIRT

In random-dyed 3 ply yarn and with size 2¼ mm. needles, cast on 30 sts. and work 3 rows in g.st. Change to s.s. and work 25 more rows, or until long enough to reach from waist to mid-calf. (i.e. not quite full-length.)
Next row: (k.1, k2tog.) 10 times.

Cast off p.wise. Sew up the back seam, gather the top edge and sew round the waist.

OVER-DRESS

Using the same needles and mid-purple yarn, cast on 36 sts. and work 4 rows in g.st. (beginning at the lower edge), then continue in s.s. for 6 more rows. (If you wish, introduce a few rows of rev. s.s. among these 6.) In the next k. row, change to dark-purple yarn, and work 2 more rows.
Next row: k2tog. to the end of the row (18 sts.), then work 11 more rows in s.s.

Divide the sts. into sets of 5, 8, and 5 sts. for the armholes. Work on these sets of sts. separately for 9 rows each. Work a k. row across all sts. and then cast off.

Fit this on to the body and sew up the back seam.

SLEEVES (make 2)

Use mid-purple for the cuffs and cast on 10 sts. Work 2 rows in g.st. then change to dark-purple and work 9 rows in s.s. Cast off. Sew up the side seams, slip the sleeves on to the arms and sew the dress around the armholes.

THE BROOM

2 p.c's twisted tightly together will make the broom handle. Bend the doubled ends over top and bottom and wrap tightly with brown yarn. Tie together a bundle of trimmed thin wire and attach to one end of the handle with a length of brown yarn.

THE CAT

Fig 4 shows the p.c. frame used for the cat. You will need about 4 p.c's and the frame should be slightly padded and wrapped to give the shape.

Using dark charcoal yarn and 2 mm. needles cast on 10 sts. and work in rev. s.s. for 6 rows. Cast on 4 sts. at the beg. of next row and work straight for 8 rows. Cast off 4 sts. at the beg. of next row and work straight for 6 rows. Cast off.

Slip the knitted cover over the padded body; sew over the head first, and run a thread around the neck to gather in. Stitch down the chest and gather a thread round the back edge to fit over the hindquarters as far as the legs.

Now make 4 legs: on 5 sts., work in rev.s.s. for about 10 rows (measure for exact size). Now sew these up and attach to the top of the cat's body.

The ears can be embroidered more easily than knitted. Use double yarn and make two or three sts. leaving a tiny loop with each one, then take several sts. into these loops, over and over, until large enough. Make the tail from a crochet chain using a fine hook and 3 strands of yarn. Embroider the eyes in green and sew on some long white whiskers.

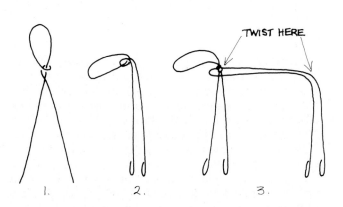

fig 4

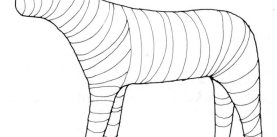

THE CAT, SLIGHTLY PADDED AND WRAPPED

Rumpelstiltskin

This is the fairy character who, every night, spun heaps of straw into gold so that the young maiden could marry the king. She then found herself in the difficult position of having to guess his name. Here he is dressed in bright colours, each side of him different, as his character shows distinct traces of both charity and malevolance! He wears tights, a longish striped, multi-coloured tunic and a close-fitting hat with a pom-pon on top. His long hair and beard are the way he is usually represented, see photo on page 21.

MATERIALS

Needles: 2 mm., 2¾ mm. and 4 mm.
Yarns: small amounts of dark and light purple, orange, yellow and red 3 ply yarns for the clothes and white 3 ply for the hair and beard. Pink and blue lengths for the features.

TROUSERS

Using orange and yellow yarns and size 2 mm. needles, begin each leg as for the prince's breeches and boots on page 8, but working 32 rows in the same colour instead of 25 rows, and draw the last row up to form the toe.

TUNIC

The front and back are the same.

With 2 mm. needles, cast on 12 sts., beg. at top and work 20 rows in s.s. (striped in 5 bands of 4 rows each). Change colour on a k. row, then work 5 rows of single rib. Cast off in rib and make another piece in the same way.

Place the 2 pieces R.S. tog. and make 2 or 3 sewing sts. on each side of the shoulder seam, allowing enough room for the head to go through the opening.

With R.S. facing, pick up 14 sts. from the base of the 3rd stripe (i.e. from the shoulder) to the base of the 3rd stripe on the other side, along the side edge of the knitting. This is for the sleeve. Begin with a p. row, and work 7 (striped) rows in s.s.
8th row: (k2tog., k.1) 4 times, k2tog.
9th row: p.
Cast off, and work the other side in the same way.

Fold the garment R.S.'s together and sew sleeve and side seams. Fit the tunic on to the figure and sl.st. the welt to the top of the legs, or leave free.

HAT

With 2 mm. needles, cast on 28 sts., being with a k. row and work in rev.s.s. for 2 rows, then change colour and work in s.s. (begin with a p. row) for 5 rows.
Next row: (k2tog.) 14 times.
Next row: p.
Next row: (k2tog.) 7 times.

Thread these 7 sts. on to a length of yarn and gather up, using the same yarn to sew up the 2 edges for the back seam. Make a pom-pon of contrasting yarn and sew this to the top.

HAIR

With white yarn and size 2 mm. needles cast on 18 sts. and work in single rib for 7 rows. Change to size 2¾ mm. needles and work 2 more rows, then change to size 4 mm. needles and work 4 more rows.
Next row: (k2tog., y.fwd.) 8 times, k2tog.
Next row: y.r.n., to make one st., then p.

Work 2 more rows in s.s. and cast off. Fold the cast off edge up, across the row of holes, to make a hem and sl.st. this in place. This is the lower edge of the hair. Sew this piece in place from one side of the face to the other leaving a bald patch on top.

BEARD AND FACE

With the same yarn and 2 mm. needles, cast on 10 sts. and work in single rib for 1 in (5 cm). Now dec. one st. at each end of every alt. row until only 2 sts. rem. K2tog. and darn the end into the beard.

Embroider the large pink nose and blue eyes, then sew the beard in place, placing a couple of sts. into the hair at each side.

Sew the hat on to the head all the way round.

OPPOSITE
The troll and Rumplestiltskin plot mischief under the pom-pon bush.

The troll

The troll is a Scandinavian-type creature, sadly mis-shapen, who lives in mountains and under bridges. Remember the story of Billy-Goat Gruff? This one has blue skin to make him appear less human! The body framework will have to be adapted somewhat, but Fig 5 gives the rough size and shape of the figure without clothes. Pad and wrap it to form this bulky appearance, and make a blue skin cover instead of a pink one. The (bare) blue feet and breeches are knitted all in one piece, as are the body and head covering. Over this, he wears a dark hooded waistcoat. The hands and sleeves are also made all-in-one piece, see photo on page 21.

MATERIALS

Needles: 2¼ mm.
Yarns: small amounts of 3 or 4 ply yarn in light, mid and dark blues. A small amount of white D.K. yarn for the beard and hair, and brown thick wool for the stick. Red yarn for the large nose. Small amounts for the features.
Extras: 2 p.c.'s twisted tightly together will make the long stick. Bend the doubled ends over at the top and bottom, and wrap tightly with brown yarn.

FEET AND BREECHES

With light-blue yarn and beginning at the toe end, cast on 8 sts. and work 14 rows in s.s., now change to mid-blue and work 2 rows.

Now inc. 1 st. at each end of the next 2 k. rows, (12 sts.).

Work straight until there are 14 mid-blue rows, then cast off and make another piece the same. These are the leg and breeches pieces: sew them up as far as the top of the leg, insert the legs and then continue to sew the front and back seams.

TUNIC AND HEAD COVER

With mid-blue yarn, cast on 26 sts. and work in s.s. for 8 rows. Divide for the armholes as follows: work on the first 7 sts. for 7 rows, then break off the yarn and join to the next section. Work on these 12 sts. for 7 rows. Break the yarn off again and work on the last 7 sts. for 7 rows, then p. across all 26 sts. and then p.

one more row. Change to light-blue and p. the next row.

Next row: (k.2, k2tog.) 6 times, k.2.

Work 9 more rows in s.s. and draw the last row up on to a thread to form the top of the head.

Sew down the back from the top of the head to the waist, then run a gathering thread round the neck and draw up firmly. Sew the lower edge of the tunic to the breeches.

BEARD, HAIR AND FACE

Using 2 mm. needles and white D.K. yarn, cast on 5 sts. and knit 5 rows in moss st. then cast off. Sew the beard on to the bottom of the face, pulling the two

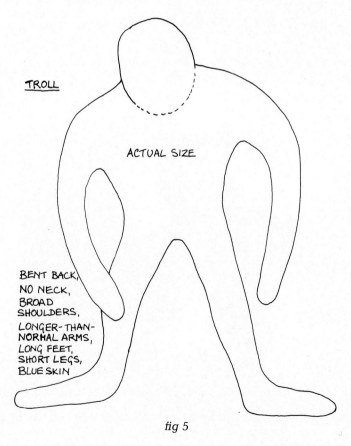

TROLL

ACTUAL SIZE

BENT BACK,
NO NECK,
BROAD
SHOULDERS,
LONGER-THAN-
NORMAL ARMS,
LONG FEET,
SHORT LEGS,
BLUE SKIN

fig 5

sides up towards the ears. Embroider the hair with the same yarn, then embroider the features.

SLEEVES (make 2)

Cast on 12 sts. (mid-blue) and work 14 rows in s.s. On the 15th row, p. instead of k. Change to light-blue yarn and work 3 rows in s.s. beginning with a p. row. Next row: (k2tog., k.3) twice, k2tog., (9 sts.).

Continue in s.s. for about 13 rows, or until the required length. Do not cast off, but draw the sts. up and sew the side seam, slip on to the arm and stitch to the tunic armhole.

HOODED WAISTCOAT

Begin with the back piece, and with dark-blue yarn cast on 16 sts. and work 20 rows in s.s.
Row 21: (k2tog., k.5) twice, k2tog.
Row 22: p. 13.
Row 23: k2tog., k.4, k2tog., k.3, k2tog.
Row 24: p. 10.

Break off the yarn and leave these sts. on a spare needle or stitch-holder. For the right front, cast on 10 sts. and work in s.s. except for the last 2 sts. in every p. row which should be knitted. Continue straight for 20 rows.
Row 21: k.8, k2tog.
Row 22: p. 7, k.2.
Row 23: k.7, k2tog.
Row 24: p. 6, k.2.

Break off yarn and slip these sts. on to a stitch holder.

For the left front, work as for right front except that the 2 g.sts. should be worked at the *beginning* of every p. row instead of at the end. Reverse all shapings.

Now place all the stitches held on stitch-holders, in order, on to one needle and k. across R. front, back, and L. front, beginning as follows:
Next row: cast off 4 sts., k. to end.
Next row: cast off 4 sts., p. to last 2 sts., k.2.

Work on these 18 sts. for the hood for 12 more rows, keeping a border of g.st. at each edge. Cast off, fold the hood in half across the top and sew together. Sew half-way up the side edges, leaving the open part for the arms.

The horse

It is quite important to spend some time on the horse's framework, as this is the largest of our animals and must take the weight of a knight in full armour! Use plenty of p.c.'s (allow 16 to 20), pad him carefully and wrap very firmly with yarn before making the cover. Remember that the cover adds something to the height and bulk of the horse. Aim for an upright stance, long slender legs and a not-too-fat body.

The padding should begin at the head-end: gently bandage the wire frame with long narrow strips of padding, making it bulkier around the shoulders, chest and hindquarters. Do not pad the legs except for the tops (see Fig 6), but use the wrapping/binding yarn to separate the hindquarters under the tail. The legs should be wrapped with yarn to make them strong and smooth, but should remain slender.

The trappings worn during jousting were more for identification purposes than anything else as the colours and designs matched those of the rider, but for us, they serve the dual purpose of hiding a less-than-perfect model. They are, of course, optional, and can be made in any colour and design you choose. You may find that a row-counter would be useful, see photo on page 26.

MATERIALS

Needles: 1½ mm., 2¼ mm., 2¾ mm. and 3 mm., and a small crochet hook.
Yarns: 25 gm. ball of 4 ply in main body-colour, small amounts for the mane and tail, and a bright colour for the trappings and harness and white yarn for the saddle (4 ply). Blue and yellow 4 ply for the horse's coat. Black yarn for the hooves.
Extras: one gold or silver button to decorate horse's coat.

KNITTED COVER

The two forelegs and underbody gusset are made in 3 separate pieces; the back legs and body are made in 2 separate pieces which are then joined so that the head and neck are a continuation of these, (see Fig 7).

FORELEGS (make 2)

Use 2¾ mm. needles and begin with black yarn for the hooves, cast on 8 sts. and work 4 rows in s.s. Change to body colour and inc. 1 st. at both ends of next row. (10 sts.). Work 13 more rows, then inc. again as before, and again on the 23rd row (14 sts.).

P. one more row and then cast off 2 sts. at beg. of next 2 rows. Dec. 1 st. at both ends of next and every foll. k. row until only 2 sts. rem. Cast off.

Sew the legs up and slip them on to the framework with the points to the outside and the seams inside.

RIGHT BACK LEG

* Cast on 8 sts. with black yarn and work 4 rows in s.s.
Change to body-colour and inc. 1 st. at both ends of next row. (10 sts.).
Work 9 more rows (14 in all).
15th row: inc. 1 st. at each end of row, also on 19th, 21st and 23rd rows, (18 sts.). Purl alt. rows.
25th row: inc. in 1st st. k.8, M1, k.8, inc. in last st.
26th row: p.
27th row: inc., k.9, M1, k.10, inc.
28th row: p., (24 sts.) *.

At this point, you can add extra rows to make the legs longer if you need to. You should have reached the top of the leg.
Next row: cast off 5 sts., k. to end.
Next row: cast off 3 sts., p. to end.
Next row: (k.3, inc. in next st.) 3 times, k.4
Next row: p.
Next row: (k.4, inc. in next st.) 3 times, k.4.
Next row: p.
Next row: (k.5, inc.) 3 times, k.4.
Next row: p.
Next row: (k.6, inc.) 3 times, k.4, (28 sts.).
Begin shaping to turn on to the back:
Next row: p.2 tog., p. across rest of sts. until you reach the last st. Leave this on the L.H. needle, turn, and k. back.

Repeat this procedure, leaving one extra st. on the L.H. needle at the end of every p. row (remembering

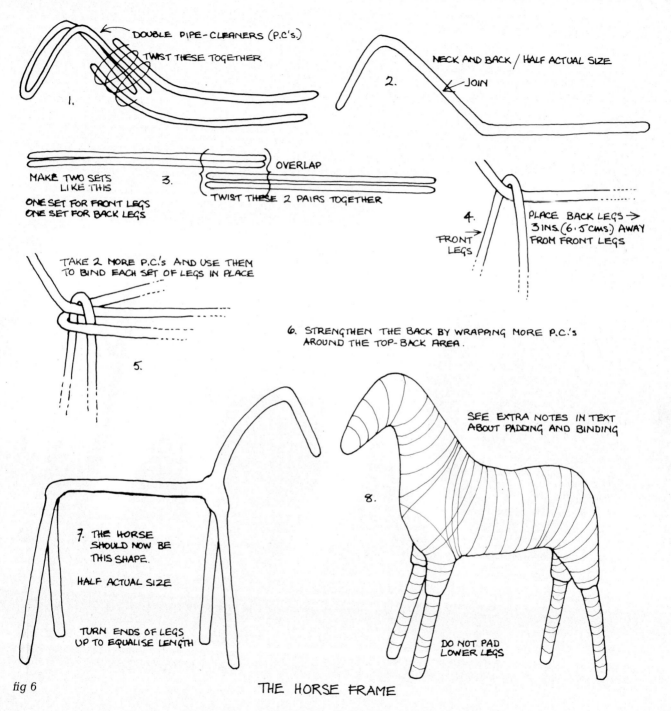

DOUBLE PIPE-CLEANERS (P.C.'s.)

TWIST THESE TOGETHER

1.

2. NECK AND BACK / HALF ACTUAL SIZE

JOIN

MAKE TWO SETS LIKE THIS

ONE SET FOR FRONT LEGS
ONE SET FOR BACK LEGS

3.

OVERLAP

TWIST THESE 2 PAIRS TOGETHER

4.

FRONT LEGS

PLACE BACK LEGS →
3 INS (6.5 CMS.) AWAY
FROM FRONT LEGS

TAKE 2 MORE P.C.'s AND USE THEM
TO BIND EACH SET OF LEGS IN PLACE

5.

6. STRENGTHEN THE BACK BY WRAPPING MORE P.C.'s
AROUND THE TOP-BACK AREA.

SEE EXTRA NOTES IN TEXT
ABOUT PADDING AND BINDING

8.

7. THE HORSE
SHOULD NOW BE
THIS SHAPE.

HALF ACTUAL SIZE

TURN ENDS OF LEGS
UP TO EQUALISE LENGTH

DO NOT PAD
LOWER LEGS

fig 6

THE HORSE FRAME

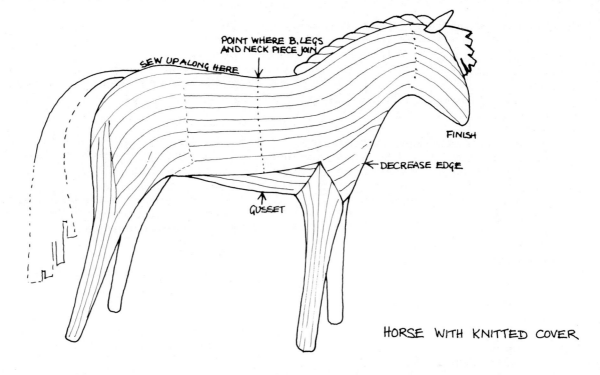

POINT WHERE B.LEGS AND NECK PIECE JOIN

SEW UP ALONG HERE

FINISH

DECREASE EDGE

GUSSET

HORSE WITH KNITTED COVER

fig 7

to p.2 tog. at the beginning) until 11 sts. rem. unworked on the L.H. side and 6 "worker" sts. on the R.H. side, 17 sts. in all). Turn and k. back, then p. across all sts. Continue without shaping for 8 more rows.
Next row: k.12, turn and p. back.
Next row: k.7, turn and p. back.
Next row: k.2, turn and p. back.

Work 2 complete rows across all these sts. and then leave them on a spare needle until the left leg has been made.

LEFT BACK LEG

Work as for right leg from * to *.
Next row: cast off 3 sts. at beg. of row, k. to end.
Next row: cast off 5 sts. at beg. of row, p. to end.
Next row: k.4 (inc. in next st., k.3) 3 times. Purl alternate rows.
Next row: k.4 (inc., k.4) 3 times.
Next row: k.4 (inc., k.5) 3 times.

OPPOSITE
The white horse is about to charge to the rescue of the princess.

Next row: k.4 (inc., k.6) 3 times. (28 sts.).
Now begin the back shaping as follows:
Next row: k2tog., k. to last st., leave this on L.H. needle, turn and p. back.

Repeat these 2 rows, leaving one extra st. on the L.H. needle at the end of every k. row (remembering to k2tog. at the beg.) until 11 sts. rem. unworked on the L.H. needle and 6 "workers" on the R.H. side, (17 sts. in all).
Turn and p. back. Continue without shaping for 7 more rows.
Next row: p. to last 2 sts., turn and k. back.
Next row: p. to last 7 sts., turn and k. back.
Next row: p. to last 12 sts., turn and k. back.

Work 3 complete rows and leave the sts. on the needle.

NECK AND HEAD

Slip both sets of sts. on to the same needle, back to back, and join them together by sewing (on the wrong side) along the back, from the needle to the 3 cast off sts. With the R.S. facing, cast on 10 sts., k2tog. on the centre 2 sts., k. to end.

Next row: cast on 10 sts. and p. to end.

Next row: k2tog., k. to centre 2 sts. and k. these tog., k. to last 2 sts., k2tog.

Next row: p.

Repeat the last 2 rows until there are 29 sts.

Next row: k2tog. at each end of row only.

Next row: p.

Repeat these last 2 rows once more, (25 sts.).

Next row: k.24, leave 1 st. on L.H. needle, turn and p.23, leaving 1 st. on L.H. needle. Turn, k. to last 2 sts., (leave 2 on L.H. needle) turn, p. back to last 2 sts., and leave these on L.H. needle.

Continue in this way, leaving one extra st. on L.H. needle at the end of every row until there are 8 unworked sts. at each side of the row.

Turn and knit back on 17 sts. then p. a complete row on 25 sts.

Work 4 rows straight, then dec. 1 st. at each end of next row and continue without shaping on 23 sts. for 5 more rows.

Next row: k2tog., k.8, sl 1 k2tog., psso., k.8, k2tog.

Next row: p. 19.

Next row: k2tog., k.15, k2tog.

Next row: p. 17.

Next row: k2tog., k.5, sl 1, k2tog., psso., k.5, k2tog.

Next row: p. 13.

Next row: (k2tog.) 6 times, k.1.

Gather these last sts. over the nose.

THE GUSSET

Make this after the rest of the coverings have been fitted.

Important note: the exact size of this is important to the fit of the "skin cover" and so the number of sts. and rows must be adjusted according to the size of the gap left underneath the body. Watch for these * marks and make your adjustments where they occur.

Begin at the chest end and cast on 2 sts. and work 2 rows.

Now inc. 1 st. at both ends of every k. row until there are * 8 sts. (or less).

Purl one row. Cast on * 8 (or less) sts. at beg. of the next 2 rows.

Work 2 rows straight, then dec. each side as folls:

Next row: k.1, sl 1, k.1, psso., k. to last 3 sts., k2tog., k.1.

Next row: p.

Repeat these 2 rows until * 6 sts. rem.

Continue without shaping (if necessary) until long enough and cast off.

MAKING UP

Pin the gusset in place (with the cast off edge at the rear) and sew to the tops of the forelegs.

Sew up the seams of the back legs and slip these on to the frame, pulling the head-piece over the head and drawing up the gathering thread at the nose-end. Pin all round on to the gusset and sew up with yarn and an invisible st.

EARS (make 2)

Use 1½ mm. needles, cast on 6 sts. and work in s.s. for 6 rows

Next row: k2tog., k.2, k2tog.

Next row: p.

Next row: (k2tog.) twice.

Cast off, fold in half lengthwise and sew on to the head.

TAIL

This is a long tassel which has been bound round the top part for 1 in (2.5 cm) to shape it. Fix it high up on to the horse's back end as shown, and trim so that the tassel is shorter on the underside.

MANE

Make a very thick plait long enough to reach from the base of the neck to well over the forehead. Tie it off between the ear, leaving ends of about 1 in (2 cm) hanging free to form the forelock. Sew this in place with firm back sts.

OTHER DETAILS

The white blaze can be made by knitting a small oblong of white yarn and sewing it down the centre of the face. White socks can also be made in this way and sewn on afterwards. The eyes are large and dark: sew them well up on the head as shown.

THE HARNESS AND TRAPPINGS

The bridle and reins are made of short lengths of

crochet chain, and a length of knitted cast-on and cast-off stitches. These short lengths are then sewn together and on to the horse's head. The blue decoration on the reins are small oblongs of g.st. made on 20 sts. and 6 rows (size 2 mm. needles) and these are then sewn on to the reins.

THE HORSE'S BLUE AND YELLOW COAT

Using 4 ply yarn and 3¼ mm. needles, work from the chart as shown on page 29, Fig 8. The white saddle is knitted into the coat, and has been outlined with a line of yellow chain st.

The little stirrups to keep the knight's feet in place are simply chained loops which are sewn firmly into the corners of the saddle patch on the horse's coat.

The horse's coat is made in two pieces which are then sewn together along the top edges. Sew down

the back edges from * to * leaving the rest open for the tail. You may need to gather this hole up with a running thread to fit on to the back. Leave the front edges open, and fasten at the neck with a gold or silver button for decoration.

THE WHITE HORSE'S SADDLE

Use 4 ply yarn and size 2¼ mm. needles.
Cast on 8 sts. and work in g.st. Work 1 row, then inc. 1 st. at each end of 2nd row, knit the 3rd row, and on the 4th row inc. again as on the 2nd, (12 sts.).
Work straight for 3 in (7.5 cm) from the beg.
Dec. 1 st. at each end of next 2 alt. rows, (8 sts.) then cast off 2 sts. at beg. of next 2 rows. Continue on the rem. 4 sts. for the girth, until this is long enough to pass under the body to the other side of the saddle.
Make the stirrups as for the blue and yellow coat.

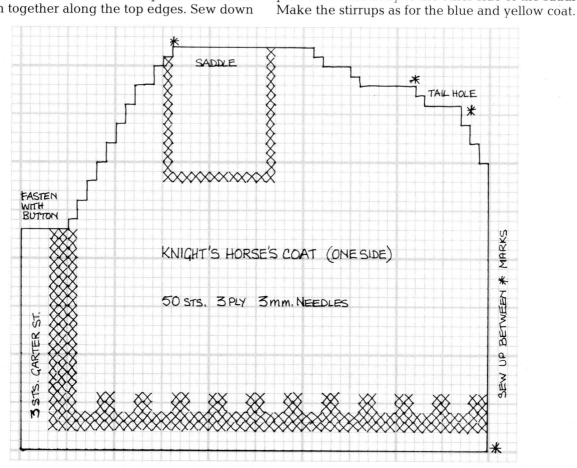

fig 8

29

The unicorn

This beautiful and mythical creature is more the size of a pony than a horse, and differs from the latter in several other ways, (see Fig 9). Apart from its spiral horn, it has a goat's beard, cloven hooves like a deer, and a lion's tail. This knitted version has hooves of gold as they are too small to show the cloven effect, see photo on page 33.

MATERIALS

Needles: 2 mm. and 2¾ mm., and a small crochet hook to hook the mane into the neck.

Yarn: 4 ply cream or white (less than 20 gms) and tiny amounts of pink and blue yarns, and metallic gold for the hooves. Some fine glitter yarn may be knitted in for the horn, and into the mane.

For the frame; about 11 p.c.'s, padding and thick white yarn for wrapping, (see Fig 10).

FRONT LEGS (make 2)

* Using 2 mm. needles and gold yarn for the hooves,

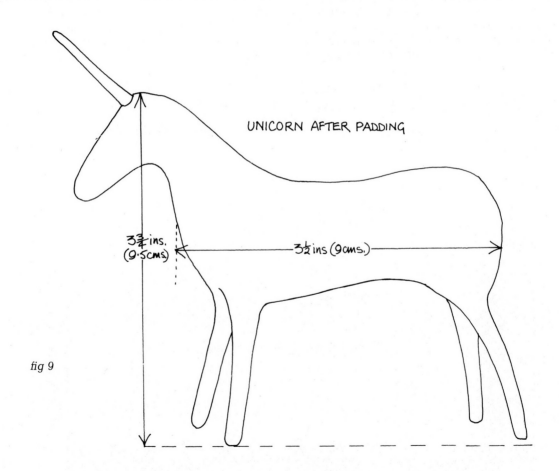

UNICORN AFTER PADDING

3¾ins. (9.5cms)

3½ins (9cms.)

fig 9

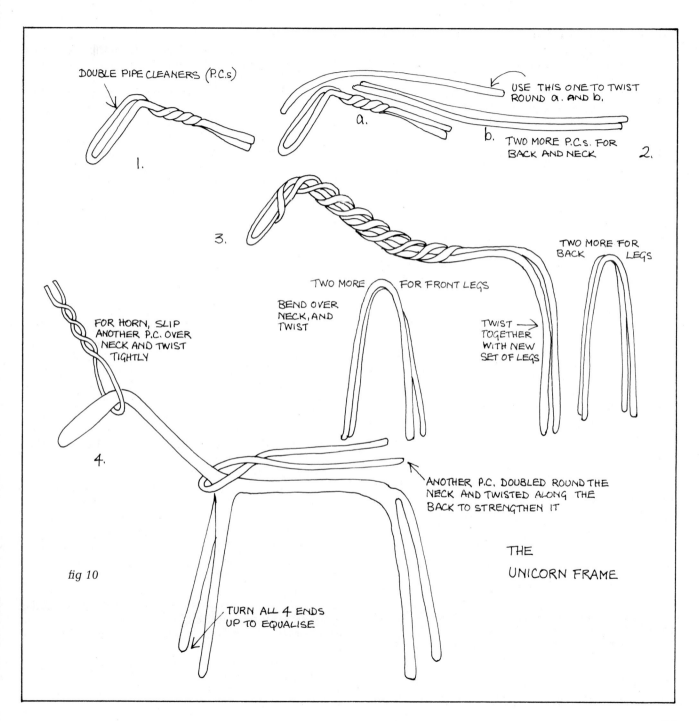

DOUBLE PIPE CLEANERS (P.C.s)

1.

USE THIS ONE TO TWIST ROUND a. AND b.

a.

b. TWO MORE P.C.s. FOR BACK AND NECK

2.

3.

TWO MORE FOR BACK LEGS

TWO MORE FOR FRONT LEGS

BEND OVER NECK, AND TWIST

TWIST TOGETHER WITH NEW SET OF LEGS

FOR HORN, SLIP ANOTHER P.C. OVER NECK AND TWIST TIGHTLY

4.

ANOTHER P.C. DOUBLED ROUND THE NECK AND TWISTED ALONG THE BACK TO STRENGTHEN IT

THE UNICORN FRAME

fig 10

TURN ALL 4 ENDS UP TO EQUALISE

cast on 8 sts. and k.4 rows in g.st, then change to white yarn and k.1 row.

Change to size 2¾ mm. needles and work in s.s. * for 12 more rows.

Now cast on 2 sts. at beg. of next 2 rows. Cast off. Sew up the seams and slip the leg-coverings in place, turning the seam towards the back.

BACK LEGS (make 2)

Work from * to * as for front legs then work for 16 more rows, and finish in the same way as for front legs.

BODY-COVER

Use size 2¾ mm. needles and white yarn, and begin at the nose end.

Cast on 12 sts. and work in s.s. for 2 rows, then inc. at each end of every k. row until there are 18 sts., ending with a p. row. Now make a hole for the horn (you may have to adjust the placing of this).

Next row: inc. in 1st st., k.7, cast off 2, k.7, inc. in last st.

Next row: p. 9, turn and cast on 2 sts., turn and p. 9.

Continue increasing in 1st and last sts. until there are 24 sts. then p. the next row.

SHAPE NECK

Inc. in 1st st., k.13, leave 10 sts. on L.H. needle, turn and p. 4. Turn and k.6, turn and p. 8, turn and k.10, turn and p. 12, turn and k.14, turn and p. 16, turn and k. to last st., inc. 1 st. Now p. across all sts.

Continue to inc. as before until there are 30 sts., then work straight for 9 more rows.

Next row: k2tog., (k.12, k2tog.) twice.

Continue without shaping for 12 rows.

Next row: inc. in 1st st., (k. 12, inc.) twice.

Next row: k.18, turn, leaving 12 sts. on L.H. needle, p. 6, turn and k.9, turn and p. 12, turn and k.15, turn and p. 18, turn and k. to the end of the row. Now p. one more row.

Next row: k2tog. across all sts. (15 sts.).

Next row: p. 15.

Gather these 15 sts. on to the attached yarn and draw up.

MAKING UP

1. First attach the leg-coverings, keeping the seams of the front ones towards the back, and those on the back ones towards the insides. Stitch the top edges to the body-padding, pulling them up high on to the body with the stitches.

2. Gather the nose-end (i.e. the cast on edge) of the body-covering and secure with one or two stitches, then sew neatly along the under-head/neck seam as far as the increases. This is the lower point of the chest, at the top of the two front legs.

3. Slip this part on to the frame, slipping the horn through the hole in the head part. Fit it snugly on to the head and chest, and pull the back curve over the back end of the body. Bring the two gathered edges together under the body at the top of the two back legs, and pin in position. Draw the edges together under the rest of the body, round the front legs, and pin. Sew neatly in position.

4. The horn should now be trimmed to about 1¼ in (3 cm) long and a cover knitted using a fine 3 ply yarn or a fine metallic yarn. Use fine size 2 mm. needles and cast on about 8–10 sts. and knit the length of the horn, tapering towards the end. Sew, from the point downwards, inserting the horn when only about half has been sewn up so that the lower half can be sewn and shaped "in situ". Sew firmly in position.

5. The ears are made from the same yarn as the body, using fine needles on about 5 sts. Work 4 rows of s.s. then k2tog., k.1, k2tog., and on the next row, p. 3, then k2tog., k.1 and cast off.

6. The tail should be more like a lion's tail than a horse's and so can be a knitted strip with a tassel sewn on to the end. Sew it well up on to the top of the rump.

7. The mane is made from short lengths of yarn hooked through the sts. along the top of the neck. Make this as thick as possible, and if it will not lie down as a mane should, it is probably better to allow it to stand up.

8. The beard, like a goat's, is just a cluster of threads hooked underneath the chin.

9. Embroider the eyes and pink nostrils as shown.

The dragon

In spite of great efforts on my part to make a really fearsome dragon, this dear little harmless creature emerged, and now the other characters are by no means afraid of him, as they were meant to be! However, I feel that he fits into the scene rather well, and he is not difficult to make. As frame sizes may differ in the making, use a tape-measure to check measurements at all stages, and alter the pattern accordingly, see photo on page 37.

MATERIALS

Needles: 1½ mm., 2¼ mm. and 2¾ mm. needles.
Yarns: about 20 gms. bright orange 3 or 4 ply, glittery yarn for the eyes.
For the frame: about 14 p.c.'s, sticky-tape, small pliers, strong bendable wire about 14 in (36 cm) long, padding.
Extras: 2 large cup-shaped sequins and 2 small glass beads for the eyes.

THE FRAME

(These numbers refer to those in Fig 11.)
1. Take 2 p.c.'s, twist them together, fold in half at right angles as shown.
2. 2 more p.c.'s twisted together 1½ in (4 cm) from the left.
3. Place this twist at * in diagram No. 1, and twist short ends round neck.
4. Strengthen back and neck with 2 more p.c.'s laid alongside and twisted.
5. Use 2 p.c.'s double, fold in half, place over body at base of neck for front legs and wrap round to hold in place. Twist legs to strengthen, and turn ends up short.
6. Use 2 more p.c.'s and do the same for the back legs, but make them shorter than the front.
7. Bow the legs wide apart and stand evenly.
8. Lengthen tail by twisting 2 p.c.'s tog., and wrapping one end round the end of the body.* Dragon frame should now measure about 9½ in (24 cm) from base of neck to tip of tail.
9. Lengthen head by folding 2 more p.c.'s in half and overlap on to neck by ¾ in. (2 cm) and bind in place with sticky-tape.

10. Bandage whole frame with long narrow strips of padding, making it thicker round the chest. Wrap in place with yarn.

KNITTED COVER (main piece)

Begin at the nose, and with size 2¼ mm. needles cast on 12 sts. and work in g.st. for 4 rows, then work 3 rows in s.s.
Row 8: inc., k.5, inc., k.4, inc., (15 sts.).
Row 9: p.
Row 10: inc. in every alt. st. to make 22 sts.
Row 11: k.
Row 12: work in moss st. for 10 rows.
Row 22: work in double moss st. for 6 rows.
Row 28: (k2tog., work 8 sts.) twice, k2tog., (19 sts.).
 Keeping the patt. correct, continue to the base of the neck (about 28 more rows).
Row 57: inc. in 1st st., (work 8 sts. inc.) twice, (22 sts.).
 Work 2 more rows.
Rows 60 & 61: inc. 1 st. at each end of row.
 Continue in double moss st. for 12 more rows on these 26 sts.
Row 74: dec. one st. at each end of this and every 4th row until 12 sts. rem.
 Work 13 more rows on these 12 sts., still in double moss st.
Cast on 3 sts. * at beg. of next 2 rows and change to single moss st.
Work 4 rows without shaping on these 18 sts.
Dec. one st at each end of next and every foll. 4th row until 10 sts. rem., and continue in moss st. until this is nearly long enough to reach the tip of the tail, then dec. 1 st. at each end of alt. rows until there are 2 sts. left. Cast off.
 Gather the cast on sts. on to a thread and draw up tightly. Sew the head up for about 1½ in (4 cm) and sew up the same length at the tail end. Slip both ends on to the frame, leaving the yarn uncut so that sewing can continue later.

LEGS AND UNDERSIDE GUSSET

Begin at the neck end, and with size 2¾ mm. needles cast on 2 sts. Work in s.s., inc. 1 st. at each end of every alt. row until there are 12 sts.

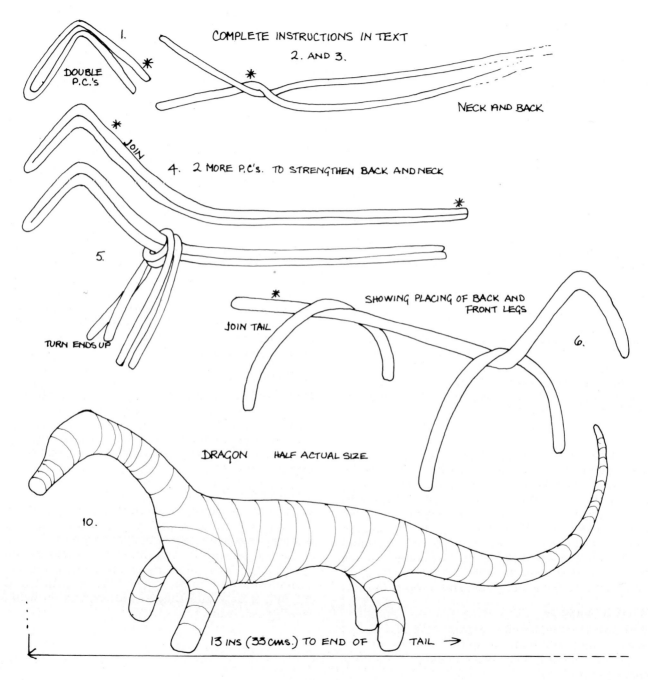

1. DOUBLE P.C.'s

COMPLETE INSTRUCTIONS IN TEXT
2. AND 3.

NECK AND BACK

JOIN

4. 2 MORE P.C's. TO STRENGTHEN BACK AND NECK

5.

TURN ENDS UP

JOIN TAIL

SHOWING PLACING OF BACK AND FRONT LEGS

6.

DRAGON   HALF ACTUAL SIZE

10.

13 INS (33 CMS.) TO END OF   TAIL →

fig 11

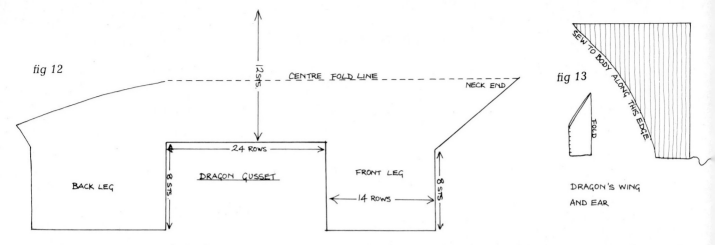

fig 12

CENTRE FOLD LINE

NECK END

12 STS

24 ROWS

DRAGON GUSSET

BACK LEG

FRONT LEG

8 STS

8 STS

14 ROWS

fig 13

SEW TO BODY ALONG THIS EDGE

FOLD

DRAGON'S WING

AND EAR

Cast on 8 sts. at beg. of next 2 rows, (28 sts.).
Work 12 more rows, then cast off 8 sts. at beg. of next 2 rows. Continue in s.s. for 24 rows, or until this piece is long enough to reach the back legs.

For the back legs, cast on 8 sts. at beg. of next 2 rows.

Next row: k. 13, k2tog., k.13.

P. alt rows and dec. 1 st. in the centre of every k. row until 21 sts. rem.
[Note: on every alt. decrease row, there will be an uneven number of sts at each side of the decrease sts.]

Cast off 8 sts. at beg. of the next 2 rows, then cast off the last 5 sts.

Fold the 4 legs in half (downwards) R.S. together, and sew up the leg seams. Turn R.S., out and slip these on to the dragon framework, pinning the neck point and the 2 sides in position. Twist the leg seams slightly towards the back. Match up the edges of the upper and lower pieces and pin together along both sides. These must be sewn up while on the framework, from the R.S., so care must be taken to make the sts. as invisible as possible. Pin the 3 extra sts. underneath the base of the tail, and sew (see Fig 12).

WINGS (make 2)

With size 1½ mm. needles, cast on 4 sts. and work 4 rows in single rib. Now inc. at the beg. of every alt. row until there are 14 sts. Work 1 more row and then cast off in rib.

Take a piece of strong but bendable wire 7 in

(18 cm) long and fold it in half, pinching the bend with pliers and gently twisting the rest together. Bend this piece into a right angle, and lay this alongside the right angle of the knitted piece. Using the same yarn, bind the wire to the edge of the knitting, covering the wire completely with yarn. Sew these wings to each side of the body at the shoulders, (see Fig 13).

EARS (make 2)

With size 1½ mm. needles, cast on 8 sts. and work in s.s. for 4 rows. Dec. 1 st. at each end of every k. row until only 2 sts. rem. Cast off. Fold ears along centre line and sew up the 2 short edges, leaving the tops open. Point the ears towards the front, pin on to head and sew firmly.

EYES (make 2)

Using glittery (or other contrasting) yarn, and size 1½ mm. needles, cast on 8 sts. and work in g.st. for enough rows to make a ¾ in (2 cm) square. Cast off. Place a small piece of padding in the centre and gather the edges round the padding and press flat.

Sew these pads to each side of the head and finish off with a large cup-shaped sequin held on with a small glass bead.

OPPOSITE
The dragon: his eyes sparkle like diamonds.

fig 14

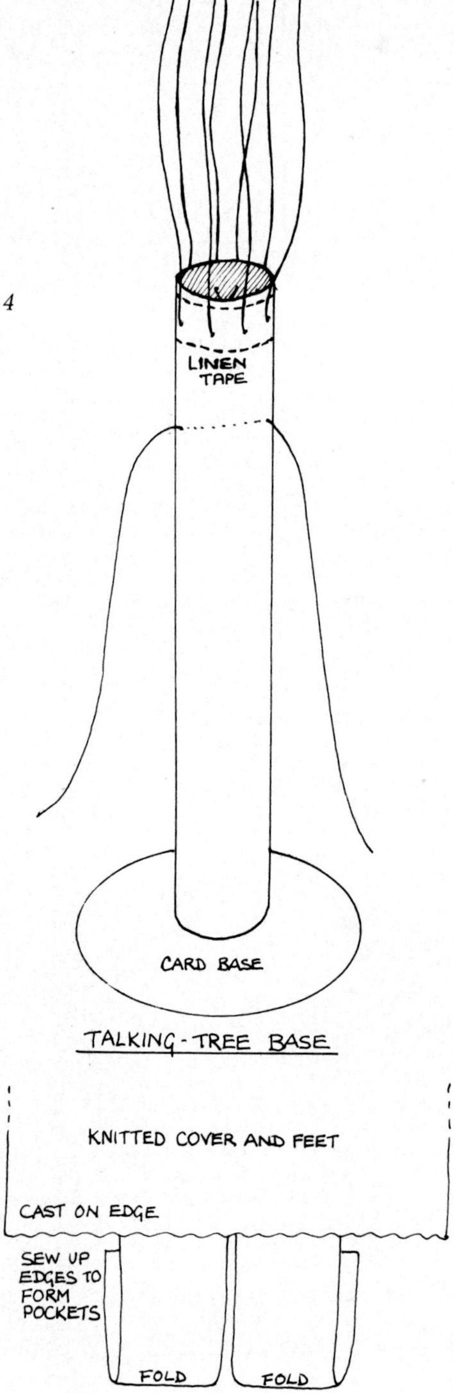

LINEN
TAPE

CARD BASE

TALKING-TREE BASE

KNITTED COVER AND FEET

CAST ON EDGE

SEW UP
EDGES TO
FORM
POCKETS

FOLD   FOLD

Talking trees

The talking trees are enchanted creatures who were changed into trees by a magical spell and are waiting to be freed from their tree-bodies. They stand about 12 in (30 cm) tall and the general pattern can be adapted in any way you choose, by colour, yarn texture, size and shape, see photo on page 39.

MATERIALS

Needles: 4 mm.

Yarn: any, but double-knitting (D.K.) or thicker, is best. Greens, browns and greys.

Card and wire base: cardboard tubes, about 9 in (23 cm) tall with a diameter of 1¼ in (3 cm). A circular piece of thick card for the stand, about 3 in (8 cm) diameter, either dark brown or dark green.

Pliable but strong wire, for each tree you will need 4 pieces, each one about 20 in (51 cm) long and one piece about 30 in (76 cm) long.

You will need a small pair of pliers, and some glue. Strong linen tape would be useful, but not essential, and a small amount of padding for the feet.

TO MAKE THE FRAME

1. Stick the base of the tube to the circle of card and allow to set (see Fig 14).

2. Make the wire branches as folls:

(a) Bend each piece of wire in half and bend the cut ends down with pliers, about ¾ in (2 cm) and twist the 2 halves together to strengthen.

(b) Make 8 small holes about ½ in (1.5 cm) down from the top edge of the tube, just big enough to allow the doubled wires to pass through and no more. Space these equally apart.

(c) Push the 4 wire pieces through the holes from one side to the other, so that there are 8 branches sticking out all around. Using the pliers, these should now be bent upwards to a vertical position for the time being. Do not tear the card while you are doing this!

OPPOSITE
The talking trees mutter among themselves about the witch's evil spells.

(d) At this point, wrap the linen tape once or twice round the top, over the wires and holes to strengthen this part.

THE TREE COVER

This is the pattern for the moss stitch tree; the cable tree will need more sts. and a cable needle.

Cast on loosely. Make a piece of knitted fabric to cover the tube (the above size will need a piece 4 in (10 cm) wide. If thick D.K. yarn is used, and size 4 mm. needles, 20 sts. will be needed. Finer yarn and/or needles will require more sts. Work in any textured st., such as double moss st. or cables, and make the nose as follows:

Next row: patt. 9 sts., then inc. 5 sts. into 1 st. by making a k.1, p.1, k.1, p.1, k.1 all into the same st.

Knit 4 or 5 rows on these 5 sts. only, then dec. back to one again. Continue along the row to the end.

Continue working to the top of the tube and then divide for the branches. Divide for 8 branches (for more than 20 sts., adjust accordingly). Keep the 20 sts. on a stitch-holder or pin, and work 8 sets of sts. individually, 4 sets of 3, and 4 sets of 2 *but* increase 1 st. at the start of each set of 2 to make 3 sts. These knitted branches should be as long as the wire branches and will enclose them when the tube is attached to the trunk. Use any st. for the branches, garter or stocking. When casting off the 3 sts., leave a long enough end of yarn to sew along each branch. When all 8 branches have been knitted, make the feet as follows:

THE FEET

Turn to the bottom of the knitted tree-cover and with the R.S. facing count 4 sts. in from the edge and pick up the next 5 sts. (i.e. from the cast-on edge) and knit 26 rows in g.st. Cast off, and pick up the next 5 sts. in the centre and knit another strip of 26 rows. Fold the strips in half and sew the two sides up, place a little padding inside the pocket thus formed and sew the cast-off edge to the trunk base (see Fig 14).

MAKING UP

Take the piece of long wire and fold it in half, bending the 2 cut ends and twisting together as before. Make holes in each side of the card tube, about 2 in (5 cm) from the top and insert the wire through the knitted cover and the card tube at the same time before sewing up.

Pin the cover on to the tube and sew up the back seam, then enclose each wire branch in its knitted cover, fastening off each one securely. Bind each wire arm (i.e. the 2 lower ones) tightly round with thick oddments of yarn until the upper arm is as thick as a pencil and the lower part slightly thinner.

Now knit 2 covers for these arms with the same yarn as before, casting on about 34 sts. and working about 6 rows in s.s., using the rev. side as the R.S. To make the piece wider at one end, k. half a row, turn and p. back. This will give 2 extra rows at one end. Position the coverings over the arms and pin in place, then sew firmly, stitching into the trunk at the "shoulder" end.

Embroider the eyes and mouth as shown.

Glue the lower edge of the trunk covering and the feet to the card base. Make a large floppy pom-pon using coarse green yarn and glue this to the top of the trunk inside the branches, pulling the ends well down over the head.

The castle

This is the enchanted castle where lives the handsome prince and his brave knights. The exact height will depend upon the materials you have available, so the instructions given here are only general ones to illustrate how this model was made. It could easily become the container for all the small characters in the book, and would be a good project for a group of people to make, see pages 43 and 46, also cover.

MEASUREMENTS

The walls are 10 in (25.5 cm) high and the gateway towers are 16 in (41 cm) to the tops of the pointed roofs. The base of the castle is the size of a large dinner plate. The two gateway towers are based on card tubes from kitchen-paper rolls, the diameters of which are 1¾ in (4.5 cm).

MATERIALS

Needles: 3¼ mm., 3½ mm. and 4mm.
Yarns: odd balls of grey and green D.K. yarn to cover the walls etc., and oddments of brown, orange and black yarns for the roof and details.
Extras: pliable card for castle walls and roofs, and thick card for the bases. A large sheet of the former will be needed, as the walls are double thickness, and the bases can be cut out of cardboard boxes. Toilet and kitchen-roll tubes for turrets and towers. Glue and staples. Thick tapestry needles (for sewing), scissors, craft knife and pins.

THE CARDBOARD SHAPE

For the base, draw round a dinner plate and cut 2 or 3 circles from 'box-card'. For the walls, decide on the height of the tower and cut 2 strips of card to encircle the base, minus a gap of about 4 in (10 cm) for the gateway. For extra strength, cut another piece to be stuck round the outside of the tower after the base and inside wall have been assembled. The diagram explains how these should be put together. Another narrow strip should be cut from spare card to go round the top edge as shown. Stick this in place and strengthen with staples too.

Cut two tall towers to go at each side of the gateway and make six small turrets as shown in the lower diagram. Do not stick these in position yet, (see Fig 15).

THE GATEWAY TOWERS (make 2)

Use a fairly thick D.K. yarn and size 4 mm. needles. cast on 26 sts. and k.24 rows of g.st. then change to s.s. and make the reverse side the R.S. Work 25 rows in rev.s.s.

Begin the window: with R.S. facing, p.8, (k.1, p.1) for 10 sts., p.8.

Next row: (W.S.) k.8, (p.1, k.1), for 10 sts., k.8.

Next row: (R.S.) p.8, k.1, p.1, join in black yarn, k.6 in black, weaving in grey behind these 6 sts. then in grey – k.1, p.1, p.8.

Next row: (W.S.) k.8, p.1, k.1, change to black p. 6, change to grey, p.1, k.1, k.8

Work these last 2 rows 5 more times (12 rows of window) then dec. one black st. at each side on every 2 rows, leaving off the moss st. edges. Work 12 rows plain then make a set of small windows above as follows:

Next row: R.S. p.6, 2 black (4 grey, k.2 black) to last 6 sts., p.6 grey.

Next row: k.6 grey, (p.2 black, k.4 grey) to last 8 sts., k.2 black, k.6 grey.

Work 6 of these rows in all then change to grey to continue as before.

[Note: on the R.S. on the first complete grey row above the windows, work 2 *knit* sts. above the black sts. of the previous row to avoid the colour-change showing on the right side.]

Work 6 straight rows, then 10 rows of double moss st. Cast off in rib.

Sew up the 2 long sides and slip this on to the cardboard tube. Stick with glue at the top and bottom edges.

THE WALLS

To suit all measurements and shapes, and to make the knitting both easier and more interesting, the walls have been designed in separate strips going from top to bottom. These are then sewn together into one long piece, and the length can then be determined by the size of the tower you have made.

fig 15

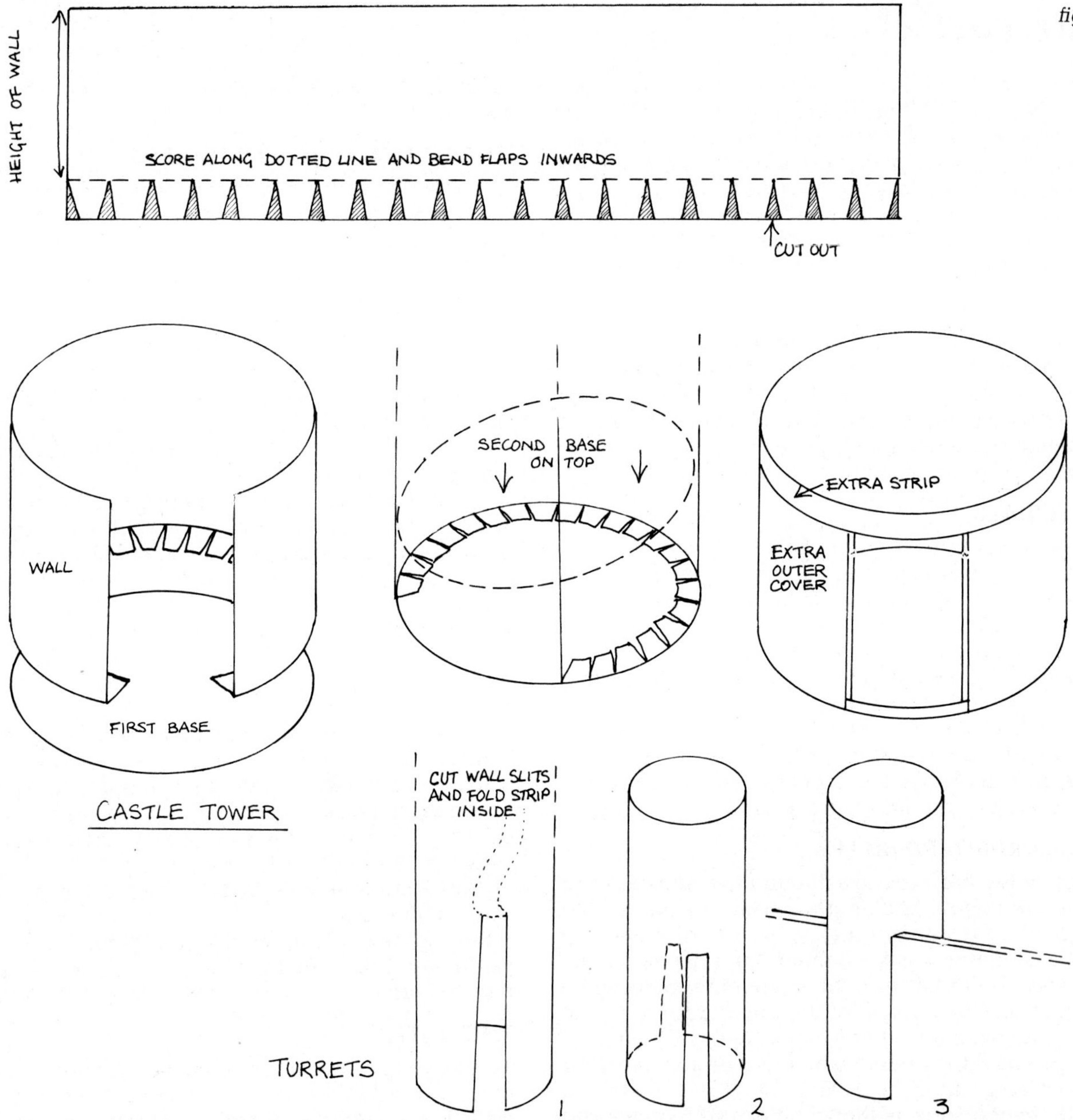

HEIGHT OF WALL

SCORE ALONG DOTTED LINE AND BEND FLAPS INWARDS

CUT OUT

WALL

FIRST BASE

CASTLE TOWER

SECOND BASE
ON TOP

EXTRA STRIP

EXTRA
OUTER
COVER

CUT WALL SLITS
AND FOLD STRIP
INSIDE

TURRETS

1   2   3

OPPOSITE
The knight, his horse and the wizard are off to battle in the forest, while the unicorn guards the princess and the castle.

If several people are working on this project, this would be an easy and painless way of covering a large surface, as long as the length of each piece (i.e. from the top of the wall to the base) was reasonably accurate. Any pieces which are a little too long can be folded over the top, and the width is not critical. The various textures/knitting stitches used will make the wall more interesting, even cables and lace patterns would be fun when combined with plain pieces. It could even be used as a sampler!

The pieces used on this castle are between 20 and 30 sts. wide, using D.K. yarn on 4 mm. needles, but there is no reason why different yarns cannot be used for this as long as the thicknesses are fairly similar. Use mossy green to suggest foliage too.

THE TURRETS (make 6)

Using the same needles and yarn, cast on 24 sts. and work in rev.s.s. for 2 in (5 cm) – about 14 rows – ending on a R.S. work (i.e. the rough side.)

Cast on 2 sts. and slide this piece on to the knob end of the needle. On the same needle, cast on another 12 sts. and work the same number of rows as the first piece. Push the two pieces together on the L.H. needle and work across both sets of sts., knitting through the back of the 2 cast-on sts. and also on the next st. As you knit these 2 pieces together, weave the broken yarn in behind the knitting; this will not show on the R.S. Work across these 26 sts. for 4 rows.

Now begin the windows as folls: break off 2 lengths of black yarn, each about 22in (56cm) long and use these for the 2 separate windows to avoid tangling.

With W.S. facing (the smooth side) work as follows:

1st row: k.5 grey, y.fwd., p.3 black, k.10 grey, y.fwd., p.3 black, k.5 grey.

2nd row: p.5 grey, yarn to back and twist round black yarn, k.3 black, p.10 grey, yarn to back and twist round black yarn, k.3 black, p.5 grey.

Work 6 of these rows in all, remembering to twist the grey and black yarns at the beg. of the 3 black sts. to avoid making a hole.

Now work across all the sts. in grey, but purl the 3 sts. above the windows (i.e. the black sts. of the previous row) on the *first* row.

Work 4 grey rows and then cast off.

Sew up the edges from the top to within 2 in (5 cm) of the lower edge, leaving the rest open to correspond with the slit in the centre of the knitting. Slip this on to the card tube, and align the 2 slits, then glue the knitting carefully in position so that no card shows. Glue round the top edge too.

POINTED ROOFS FOR GATEWAY TOWERS AND TURRETS

Although the 2 card roofs are slightly different, the same knitted cover is used for both sizes as it stretches to fit (see Fig 16). Oddments of orange and brown 3–4 ply yarns are used and pieces of bendy card, staples and glue. Size $3\frac{1}{2}$ or $3\frac{1}{4}$ mm. needles. Changes in yarn and needle sizes will produce roofs of a different size too. You may also need a crochet hook.

Cast on 40 sts. and work 2 rows in s.s.

Row 3: (k2tog., k.8) 4 times, (36 sts.)

Work three straight rows between each decrease row.

Row 7: (k2tog. k.7) 4 times, (32 sts.).

Row 11: (k2tog., k.6) 4 times, (28 sts.).

Row 15: (k2tog., k.2) 7 times, (21 sts.).

Row 19: (k2tog., k.1) 7 times, (14 sts.).

Row 23: (k2tog.) 7 times.

Next row: p.7. Break off yarn, leaving a long end.

Gather the last sts. on to the length of yarn and sew up to fit the card shape.

To neaten the edge, a tiny crochet st. has been worked in to each knit st. of the cast-on edge using a size 3 mm. hook and a simple d.c.st., but this is optional. On the 2 gateway towers, another row of chained loops has been worked for extra decoration, but this also is optional.

THE CRENELLATIONS

These are optional but add an authentic touch to the top of the castle walls, and are added as a series of long narrow strips after the walls have been covered with knitting and the turrets stuck in place on top of them. For the strip over the gateway, knit a narrow strip in rev.s.s. to stretch from one gateway tower to the other – about 8–10 sts. wide, with 10 rows in grey, 10 in black and 10 more in grey. The exact

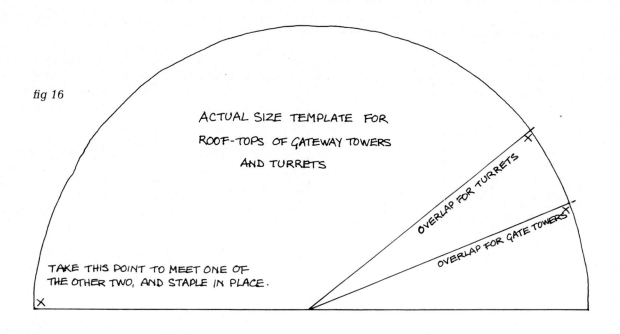

fig 16

ACTUAL SIZE TEMPLATE FOR
ROOF-TOPS OF GATEWAY TOWERS
AND TURRETS

OVERLAP FOR TURRETS

OVERLAP FOR GATE TOWERS

TAKE THIS POINT TO MEET ONE OF
THE OTHER TWO, AND STAPLE IN PLACE.

measurements will depend upon the individual castles. The small strips between the turrets are made separately (see Fig 16) and are glued on top of the knitted walls as shown.

THE DRAWBRIDGE

This is simply an oblong of card sandwiched between 2 pieces of knitting, one side in brown (any ridged pattern works well) and the other a paler colour/tone in smooth s.s. The size of the card should be large enough to fit closely inside the gate area between the 2 towers, and the bottom edge can be sewn to the edge of the base. Measure the width of your gateway and be sure to cast on enough sts. to cover the card piece. This drawbridge needed 32 sts. for a piece of card 5 in (13 cm) wide, and a fancy rib st. was used.

LARGE EYELET RIB

(you need a multiple of 6 sts. + 2 extra).
R.S. row 1. * p.2, k.4, * rep to last 2 sts., p.2.
W.S. row 2. k.2, * p.4, k.2 *, rep from * to end.

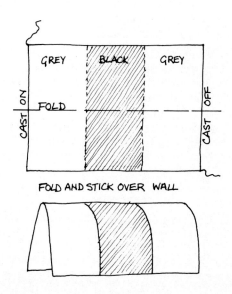

GREY   BLACK   GREY

CAST ON   FOLD   CAST OFF

FOLD AND STICK OVER WALL

Row 3: * p.2, k2tog., y.fwd. twice, s.1 1, k.1, psso., * to last 2 sts., p.2.
Row 4: k.2, * p.1, k. into 1st y.fwd. and p. into 2nd y.fwd., p.1., k.2.*

45

ORDER OF ASSEMBLY

1. Stick knitted strip over gateway.

2. Cover walls, stick along top and bottom edges. Leave a narrow strip of card showing down each edge of the gateway.

3. Cover turrets and position on walls at equal distances.

4. With a fine skewer or thick needle, punch holes at ¼ in (1 cm) intervals all the way down the bare strip of card at the sides of the gateway.

5. Cover the 2 gateway towers and sew these firmly in position through their knitted covers and into the holes of the card at each side of the gateway. Use a strong double thread (of yarn) for this, and a long needle.

6. If necessary, knit a strip to cover the *inside* of the narrow strip of card above the gateway.

7. Make the card roofs and knitted covers and stick these in place by glueing the top edges of the *towers*.

8. Make the crenellation strips to cover the top edges of the walls and stick these in place.

9. Make the drawbridge card and knitting, and fix in place.

10. For extra effect, you may wish to line the inside of the castle too, or even make a lid for it.

SMALL TREES AND BUSHES

These are perhaps the simplest of all to make.

Cover a toilet-rull tube with a simple oblong of knitting, using g.st., s.s., rev.s.s. or a textured yarn. Sew the two edges together and glue the piece in place, then add a huge, thick pom-pon of green, green/brown, russet or blossom-pink yarn. If the tree falls over easily, cut a small circle of thick card and glue this on to the base. The card tubes can be cut in half to make bushes. The pom-pons are glued to the tops.

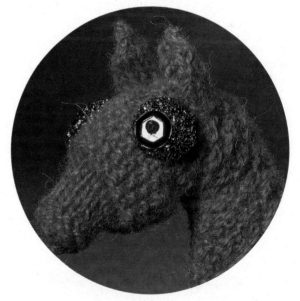

OPPOSITE
The talking trees and pom-pon bushes surround the castle while the wicked witch sweeps the battlements with her broomstick.

Typeset by Phoenix Photosetting, Chatham
Made and printed in Spain by A.G. Elkar S. Coop.
Bilbao-12.